6/30/22

Find the joy that's all around you.

Written & Compiled by: M.H. Clark
Designed by: Steve Potter

COMPENDIUM®
INCORPORATED

live inspired.®

Find your happy.

Every day is an opportunity to bring good into your life. Every day is a chance to find more happiness. You can do it in small ways: with a cup of tea, a moment of quiet, or a phone call to someone who always brings you joy. You can do it in big ways: by setting out in a bold new direction, making a positive change, or choosing to create new priorities.

Wherever you are, whatever you're doing, you can find your happy simply by deciding to look for it, because there are always good things within reach. Cultivate a habit of noticing them. Expect joy to surprise you in the most unexpected ways. Invite delight, every day, and find your happy. You'll realize it wants to find you, too.

Discover
the happiness
within you.

Happiness is not
in our circumstances,
but in ourselves.
It is not something we see,
like a rainbow, or feel,
like the heat of the fire.
Happiness is something we are.

~John B. Sheerin

Seek until you find.

Find out where joy resides... *~Robert Louis Stevenson*

Make
your own light.

Wherever you go, no matter what the weather,
always bring your own sunshine.

~Anthony J. D'Angelo

See
beauty
and
potential
everywhere.

Every moment is a golden one

for him who has the vision

to recognize it as such.

~Henry Miller

Enjoy life!

Happiness, not in
another place, but this place...
not for another hour,
but this hour.

~Walt Whitman

Cherish what you have right now.

Remember this, that very little is needed to make a happy life.

~Marcus Aurelius

Even the most ordinary day holds opportunities for happiness: a quiet moment of rest, a challenge to take on, a goal to meet, a friend to visit, a chance to try something new, to be loved, to express love. Challenge yourself to find joy in the everyday things. Make a decision to dedicate yourself to feelings that uplift you, empower you, delight you. Seek out opportunities to be happy. You'll discover them everywhere.

Day

Make today count.

I have just one day,
today, and I'm going
to be happy in it.

~Groucho Marx

Live in joy.

Learn to enjoy every minute of
your life. Be happy now. Don't wait
for something outside of yourself
to make you happy in the future.
Think how precious is the time you
have to spend, whether it's at work
or with your family. Every minute
should be enjoyed and savored.

~Earl Nightingale

Love the ordinary moments.

Being happy isn't having
everything in your life be
perfect. Maybe it's about
stringing together all
the little things.

~Ann Brashares

Put first things first.

I've got nothing to do today but smile.

~Simon & Garfunkel

Appreciate the little things.

Many people
lose the small joys
in the hope for the
big happiness.

~Pearl S. Buck

Make
time.

You should laugh every day. *~Jim Valvano*

Find the people who make your heart sing, the people whose joy is contagious, the people who bring out the best in you.

Live Happy To

Make time for these people. Build your life with them. Invite them into your days and into your heart, because when you surround yourself with people who live joyfully, their joy becomes yours too.

gether

Be radiant.

Happy people are beautiful.
They become like a mirror and
they reflect that happiness.

~Drew Barrymore

Remember the things that matter most.

This life is for loving, sharing, learning, smiling, caring, forgiving, laughing, hugging, helping, dancing, wondering, healing, and even more loving.

~Steve Maraboli

Let others
be the
source of
your delight.

Because I was more often happy for other people, I got to spend more time being happy. And as I saw more light in everybody else, I seemed to have more myself.

~Victoria Moran

Create happiness

Join with those
who sing songs,
tell stories, enjoy life...
because happiness is contagious.

~Paulo Coelho

Give joy,
receive joy.

Happiness [is] only real when shared.

~Christopher McCandless

Start something

good.

If I can see joy in your eyes then
share with me your smile.

~*Santosh Kalwar*

Live Happy By Ch...

Recognize the good wherever you may find it. Play up the glimmers of hope. Meet the world halfway with positivity, with determination, with an unstoppable spirit. And on the days when it seems the only choice you have is the choice of how you feel, choose to see possibilities, choose to think good thoughts, choose to live happy.

oice

Thoughts
become
things...
choose the
good ones!

~Mike Dooley

Put yourself
in charge of your
own happiness.

...happiness is the result of personal effort.
You fight for it, strive for it, insist upon
it, and sometimes even travel around
the world looking for it. You have to
participate relentlessly.

~Elizabeth Gilbert

Give joy a chance to find you.

Now and then it's
good to pause in our
pursuit of happiness
and just be happy.

~Guillaume Apollinaire

Make good things happen.

Happiness is not something ready made.
It comes from your own actions.

~Dalai Lama XIV

Recognize that happiness is always an option.

Why not choose joy? Why not live in joy?   *~Leo Buscaglia*

Watch
the world
with wonder.

If you look the right way, you
can see that the whole world
is a garden.

~Frances Hodgson Burnett

Your happiness may require bold changes. It may require fearlessness, perseverance, or courage. It may require starting anew. Make decisions that give happiness the space to take root in your life. This is your life, your chance to discover all that is possible, your time to look forward in joy. Follow your heart, listen to it. Find that happiness is always within reach if you're brave enough to take it.

Always

Enjoy this day,
this hour,
this minute.

Be happy for this moment.

This moment is your life.

~Omar Khayyam

Be courageous enough to change.

Wherever you are, be there totally.
If you find your here and now intolerable
and it makes you unhappy, you have
three options: remove yourself from the
situation, change it, or accept it totally.

~Eckhart Tolle

Make gladness
a priority.

The most important thing is to enjoy your life—to be happy— it's all that matters.

~Audrey Hepburn

Design this day
the way you
want it.

If you want your life to be a magnificent story, then begin by realizing that you are the author and everyday you have the opportunity to write a new page.

~Mark Houlahan

See the
good things all
around you.

The more you praise and
celebrate your life, the more
there is in life to celebrate.

~Oprah Winfrey

Look forward with hope.

Something good will come of all things yet.

~Jack Kerouac

With special thanks to the entire Compendium family.

Credits:
Written & Compiled by: M.H. Clark
Designed by: Steve Potter
Edited by: Amelia Riedler
Creative Direction by: Julie Flahiff

ISBN 978-1-935414-85-8

COMPENDIUM®
INCORPORATED

live inspired.™